JUNIOR
BIOGRAPHIES

Rita Santos

DWAYNE "THE ROCK"
JOHNSON

PRO WRESTLER AND ACTOR

Enslow Publishing
101 W. 23rd Street
Suite 240
New York, NY 10011
USA

enslow.com

WORDS TO KNOW

audience The people who watch a performance.

confidence Believing in what you can do.

demigod Someone who is half human and half god.

determined Making a decision and sticking to it.

discipline Training yourself to follow a set of rules in order to achieve a goal.

discourage To make someone not want to do something.

heritage A group's history and traditions.

professional Paid to do an activity or sport.

promoter A person who pays for and advertises an event.

scholarship Money that is awarded to someone to help pay for school.

CONTENTS

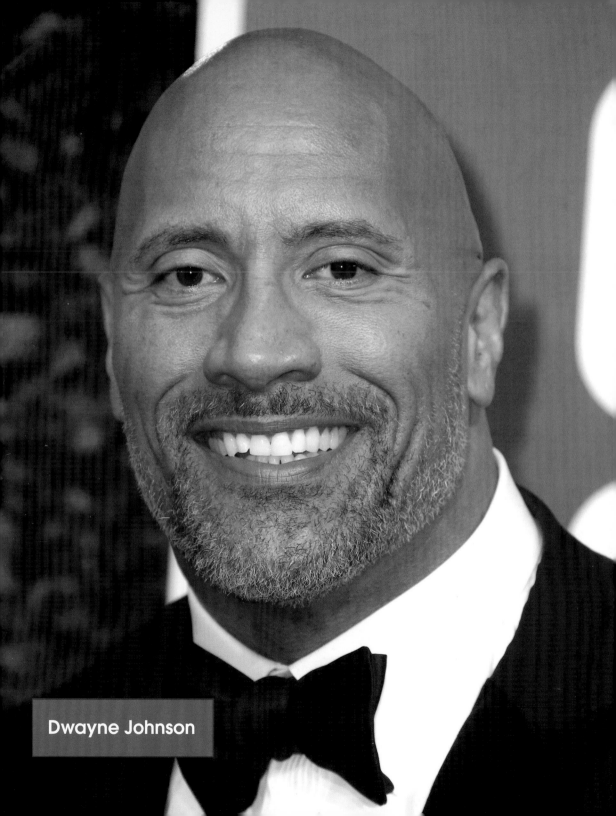

Dwayne Johnson

Sports were a big deal in the Johnson family. Young Dwayne played several sports in school, and he was good at them. His family cheered for all his teams. But there was one sport they loved most of all: wrestling.

WRESTLING HERITAGE

Dwayne's father, Rocky Johnson, was from Canada. He was a **professional** wrestler. His mother, Ata, was the daughter of the famous Samoan pro wrestler Peter Maivia. Even Dwayne's grandmother, Lia Maivia, loved wrestling. She was a famous wrestling **promoter** in Samoa. She was one of the first women to do the job. From 1982 to 1988, Dwayne's grandmother ran Polynesian Pacific Pro Wrestling.

Dwayne's grandfather, Peter Maivia (*right*), was a professional wrestler who was known as "High Chief." Here he is wrestling in 1979.

Samoa is an island in the South Pacific.

Professional wrestling is a sport that can be a lot like theater. Wrestlers will often take different names, like a stage name. They might play roles like the hero or the villain. But it is not just acting. Professional wrestlers must train very hard to be able to safely perform each move. If they aren't careful, wrestlers can injure themselves or their opponent.

LEARNING DISCIPLINE

Dwayne was born on May 2, 1972, in Hayward, California. When he was a young boy, his family moved to New Zealand

Growing up, Dwayne was very close with his mother, Ata (seen here in 2016).

for his parents' work. There he attended Richmond Road Primary School. Then the family moved to Hamden, Connecticut. Dwayne was a student at Shepherd Glen Elementary school and Hamden Middle School.

Dwayne Says:

"Not only do I think being nice and kind is easy, but being kind, in my opinion is important."

Dwayne began working out with his dad when he was a young boy. He had learned from his father and grandfather that discipline was important for athletes. Training isn't always fun, and it takes a lot of time. But Dwayne knew hard work was the way to success.

Dwayne's family moved a lot because of his father's work. For most of high school he lived in Honolulu, Hawaii. Dwayne loved living on the island. It reminded him of Samoa. His mother's **heritage** was very important to him. In the eleventh grade, the family moved again. This time they went to Bethlehem, Pennsylvania. There Dwayne was on the school's track and field, wrestling, and football teams.

Dwayne's father, Rocky, was a professional wrestler who won many championships.

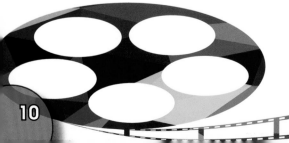

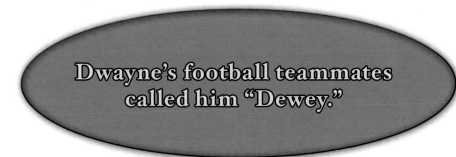

Dwayne's football teammates called him "Dewey."

ON THE TEAM

Dwayne loved wrestling. But the University of Miami offered him a **scholarship** to play football. So he moved to Miami. Dwayne was determined to give everything he had as a student and as an athlete. He earned a bachelor's degree in criminology and physiology in 1995. While he was at the university, he met his future wife, Dany Garcia.

Dwayne played defensive tackle for the Miami Hurricanes.

SUCCESS AND FAILURE

Football, like wrestling, can be a dangerous sport. Dwayne made it all the way to the national championship team for the Miami Hurricanes. Then he was injured and lost his place on the team. After Dwayne graduated he joined the Calgary Stampeders. They were a part of the Canadian Football League.

Dwayne Says:

"Success isn't overnight. It's when every day you get a little better than the day before. It all adds up."

Dwayne was cut by the Stampeders after two months. His football dreams seemed to be over. But there was another sport he wanted to try.

Dwayne returned home and asked his father to train him to wrestle. At first, Rocky did everything he could to **discourage** his son. His father wanted him to continue his football career. But Dwayne was **determined**. His heart wasn't in football. He knew he could be a champion, just like his father and grandfather.

Early in his wrestling career, Dwayne was known as Flex Kavana.

Dwayne Says:

"The road to success and greatness is always paved with consistent hard work."

A ROCKY START

Dwayne's father finally agreed to train him. Rocky was hard on his son during training. He wanted him to learn to always try his very best. His training paid off. Dwayne joined the World Wrestling Federation in 1996. He started wrestling under the name Rocky Maivia, to honor both sides of his family.

Dwayne attends the 1999 Emmys. In his early years as a wrestler, he struggled with his image.

Dwayne's wrestling nickname was "the Blue Chipper."

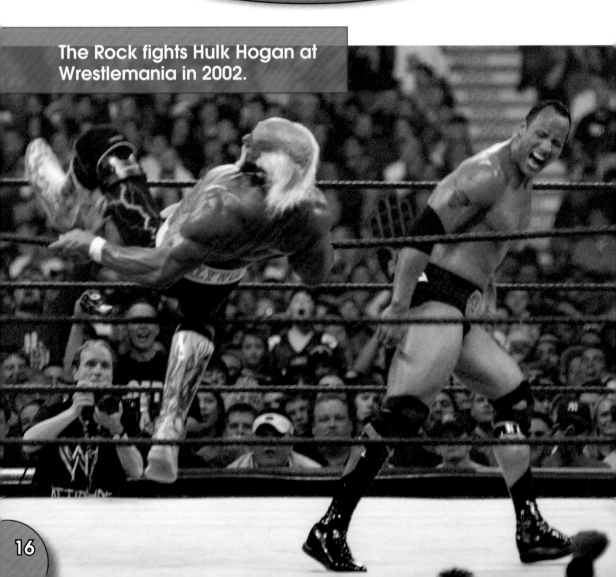

The Rock fights Hulk Hogan at Wrestlemania in 2002.

An important part of professional wrestling is entertaining the crowd before and after the wrestling matches. Dwayne loved to wrestle, but he was always unhappy with his acting performances. He was trying to be someone the **audience** would like. But the audience was also becoming unhappy with him. Fans were actually beginning to boo him! Dwayne knew he had to change something.

BE WHO YOU ARE

In 1997, Dwayne injured his knee in a match against a wrestler called Mankind. As he healed, he tried to understand why he was unhappy with his performances. Dwayne realized he wasn't being himself. He was trying to act like someone else. The audience didn't like it.

When Dwayne returned to the ring he decided to be true to himself.

Dwayne gave himself the new nickname "The Rock." His acting gained **confidence** when he began to trust himself. Fans loved the change! He became one of the most popular wrestlers of his time. He also became one of the best. He won many championship titles during his wrestling years.

CHAPTER 4
A NEW ARENA

Dwayne had made his name in the ring. Now he decided it was time to try something new. As The Rock's popularity grew, he realized that acting was one of his favorite parts of wrestling. He wanted to become an actor. He put as much effort into his acting as he did everything else. His first movie role was as the Scorpion King in *The Mummy Returns* in 2001.

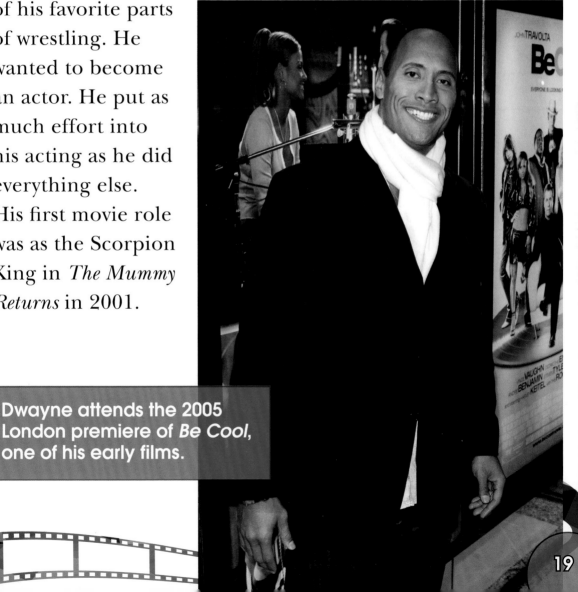

Dwayne attends the 2005 London premiere of *Be Cool*, one of his early films.

MOANA

Dwayne's dedication to his work helped make people want to cast him in movies. They knew he would do a good job. Over the years Dwayne has played many characters, but one role was extra special to him.

In 2016, Dwayne was given the chance to play the Polynesian **demigod**

Dwayne started a charity to help sick children. Here he visits with young patients at a hospital in 2009.

Maui in the Disney movie *Moana*. Samoa is a part of Polynesia. Dwayne was happy to have the chance to help share a story about his culture with the world.

Dwayne Says:

"**Blood, sweat and respect. First two you give, last one you earn.**"

Becoming High Chief

Dwayne "The Rock" Johnson has gone by many names during his career. But it's his personal titles that matter the most to him. In 2004, Dwayne was made a Samoan high chief just like his grandfather had been. Dwayne was given the name Seiuli. He was deeply honored by it.

There was still one title that was more important to Dwayne than any other. He would always be the most proud of his three daughters; Simone, Jasmine, and Tiana Gia. Of all the names he'd been called in his life, Dad would always be his favorite.

Dwayne received a star on the Hollywood Walk of Fame in 2017. His partner Lauren and daughter Jasmine attended the ceremony with him.

Timeline

1972 Dwayne is born on May 2 in Haywood, California.

1995 Earns his bachelor's degree in criminology and physiology from the University of Miami.

1996 Joins the World Wrestling Federation.

1997 Marries Dany Garcia.

1997 Daughter Simone is born.

2001 Dwayne has his first movie role in *The Mummy Returns.*

2004 Becomes a Samoan high chief.

2007 Dwayne and Dany divorce but she continues to work as his manager.

2015 Dwayne and partner Lauren Hashian have daughter Jasmine.

2016 Dwayne is cast to play Maui in Disney's *Moana.*

2018 Daughter Tiana Gia is born.

BOOKS

Chiu, David. *An Insider's Guide to Wrestling: Sports Tips, Techniques, and Strategies.* New York, NY: Rosen, 2015.

Kortemeier, Todd. *Superstars of WWE.* Minnesota, MN: Amicus Ink, 2017.

Pantaleo, Steven. *WWE: The World of The Rock.* New York, NY: DK, 2018.

WEBSITES

Samoa
easyscienceforkids.com/all-about-samoa
Learn more about Samoa.

World Wrestling Federation: Dwayne "The Rock" Johnson
www.wwe.com/superstars/the-rock
Check out photos, videos, news, and a biography of The Rock.

Index

Published in 2020 by Enslow Publishing, LLC.
101 W. 23rd Street, Suite 240, New York, NY 10011

Copyright © 2020 by Enslow Publishing, LLC.

Library of Congress Cataloging-in-Publication Data
Names: Santos, Rita, author.
Title: Dwayne "the Rock" Johnson : pro wrestler and actor / Rita Santos.
Description: New York : Enslow Publishing, 2020. | Series: Junior Biographies | Audience: Grade level for this book is 3-5. | Includes bibliographical references and index.
Identifiers: LCCN 2018048402| ISBN 9781978507678 (library bound) | ISBN 9781978508866 (paperback) | ISBN 9781978508873 (6 pack)
Subjects: LCSH: Johnson, Dwayne, 1972–Juvenile literature. | Wrestlers–United States–Biography–Juvenile literature. | Actors—United States–Biography–Juvenile literature.
Classification: LCC GV1196.J64 S27 2020 | DDC 796.812092 [B] –dc23
LC record available at https://lccn.loc.gov/2018048402

Printed in the United States of America

To Our Readers: We have done our best to make sure all website addresses in this book were active and appropriate when we went to press. However, the author and the publisher have no control over and assume no liability for the material available on those websites or on any websites they may link to. Any comments or suggestions can be sent by e-mail to customerservice@enslow.com.

Photos Credits: Cover, p. 1 Samir Hussein/WireImage/Getty Images; p. 4 Frederick M. Brown/Getty Images; p. 6 New York Post Archives/Getty Images; p. 8 Patrick Riviere/Getty Images; p. 10 Brent Perniac/SIPA/Newscom; p. 12 Collegiate Images/Getty Images; p. 14 Kurt Krieger/Corbis Entertainment/Getty Images; p. 15 Frank Micelotta Archive/Hulton Archive/Getty Images; p. 16 George Pimentel/WireImage/Getty Images; p. 19 Dave Hogan/Getty Images; p. 20 Jon Furniss/WireImage/Getty Images; p. 21 Axelle/Bauer-Griffin/FilmMagic/Getty Images; interior page bottoms (film reels) thenatchdl/Shutterstock.com.